Contents

People in the story

Harley Kirkpatrick: a journalist
Annie Shepherd: a journalist
Erik Van Delft: a businessman
Sophie Lafon: owner of a jewellery shop

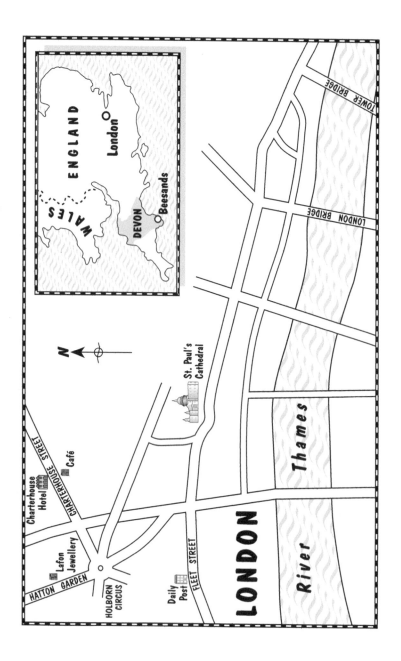

Chapter 1 *A front-page story*

'We're on the front page,' said Annie Shepherd. She smiled at Harley Kirkpatrick, and gave him a coffee and that day's *Daily Post*.

Kirkpatrick looked at the front page of the newspaper. His name and Shepherd's were there. It was their first front-page story. He felt good. Four and a half million people bought the *Daily Post* every day. He drank a little coffee and read the story quickly.

Blood diamonds

by H. Kirkpatrick and A. Shepherd

Diamonds are important for a number of countries in Africa. Diamonds buy food and doctors; they give people work, and help them get money. But in some countries people buy guns with the diamonds. We call these diamonds 'blood diamonds' because many people die from the guns. In Angola in the 1990s blood diamonds made US$3.7 billion in five years. That money bought a lot of guns. And in Angola in the 1990s a lot of people died because of these guns.

The United Nations is trying to stop blood diamonds.

'A good start to a Wednesday morning,' said Shepherd. 'A front-page story.'

Kirkpatrick looked up.

'Yes,' he said. 'Blood diamonds is an important story.'

'Yes,' she replied. 'And I've got a new story about them.'

Kirkpatrick and Shepherd worked well together. Kirkpatrick went out and asked people questions. Shepherd worked in the office; she used the computer and the Internet.

'Tell me about it,' he said.

Shepherd smiled at him again. She was twenty-seven years old, with short light brown hair and dark brown eyes. She wore blue jeans and a white shirt.

'Come over to my computer and have a look,' she said.

Kirkpatrick went over and looked at a photograph of a man on Shepherd's computer. The man's hair and eyes were dark. He wore dark trousers, a jacket and a tie and had a black bag in one hand.

'This is Erik Van Delft,' said Shepherd. 'He's thirty-six years old. Half Belgian, half African. He's in Britain now. He came into London yesterday evening from Lagos in Nigeria.'

'And who is he?' asked Kirkpatrick. 'What does he do?'

'Well, he's a businessman,' replied Shepherd. 'He buys and sells things in many countries. Some people think he also buys and sells guns . . . and blood diamonds.'

Kirkpatrick looked at Shepherd.

'I had a look on the Internet late yesterday,' she said. 'There was a lot about his business, but his name was also in a story from a South African newspaper about blood diamonds.'

'That's interesting,' said Kirkpatrick.

Shepherd gave some papers to Kirkpatrick.

'This is all from the Internet,' she said. 'The first one is the South African story. I'm going to look again today.'

'OK,' said Kirkpatrick. 'And we need to know where Van Delft is now.'

'He's at the Charterhouse Hotel, on Charterhouse Street,' said Shepherd.

Kirkpatrick laughed. 'Good work!' he said.

'This morning, I spoke to one of the people who work there,' said Shepherd. 'She's going to watch Van Delft for me. For a little money, of course.'

'*Very* good work!' said Kirkpatrick, laughing again. Then he looked at his watch. It was a quarter to ten. He stood up.

'Maybe Van Delft is still at the hotel,' he said.

'What are you going to do?' asked Shepherd. 'You can't just ask, "Do you buy and sell guns or blood diamonds?"'

Kirkpatrick took the papers.

'I'm going to read these first,' said Kirkpatrick. 'Then I'm going to watch and see where Van Delft goes.'

'Well, don't do anything stupid!' Shepherd did not look happy. Sometimes Kirkpatrick wanted a story *too* much.

Kirkpatrick put a hand on her arm.

'Of course not, Annie,' he said. 'Of course not!'

Out on the street Kirkpatrick stopped and put on his jacket. The *Daily Post* was on Fleet Street in London. At one time all the important British newspapers were on Fleet Street. But now only the *Daily Post* had an office there. The other newspapers were all in the east of London.

Fleet Street was not far from Charterhouse Street and it was a warm October day. Kirkpatrick started walking. He needed some time to think about Van Delft. And he needed to read the papers from Shepherd.

Chapter 2 *Meeting Van Delft*

There was a café across the street from the Charterhouse Hotel. Kirkpatrick went in, asked for a coffee and sat at a table near the window. He was a tall man, about thirty, with long brown hair and blue eyes. He wore jeans, a jacket, a blue shirt and light brown shoes.

He read the papers from Shepherd. The South African story was short and Van Delft's name was in it. It asked the question: 'Does this man buy and sell blood diamonds?' Kirkpatrick also learned a lot about Van Delft's business: it brought coffee, fruit and other things from Africa to Europe, and then took cars and computers back to Africa.

He waited in the café and thought about how to start a conversation with Van Delft.

He didn't have time to think of an answer. Van Delft came out of the hotel, a black bag in his hand.

Kirkpatrick drank his coffee and stood up. Van Delft turned right and started walking. Kirkpatrick took his jacket and went after him. He needed to talk to Van Delft – but how?

Van Delft walked down to Holborn Circus and then turned right into Hatton Garden. Kirkpatrick was fifty metres behind.

Hatton Garden is famous for its jewellers' shops. There are all kinds of jewellery in the shop windows – watches, diamond rings – but Van Delft didn't stop to look at them. About 200 metres down the street he opened a door and walked into a shop. *Lafon Jewellery – Paris London Antwerp*.

Kirkpatrick looked at his watch. It was half past ten. He walked up to *Lafon Jewellery* and looked in through the window. The shop wasn't open now. Van Delft and a young woman were at the back of the shop. The young woman had long dark hair. Van Delft's bag was in her hand. They went into a room and closed the door.

Kirkpatrick walked down the street. He looked in the shop windows, but every two or three seconds he looked back at *Lafon Jewellery.* No one came out. He thought again about how to start a conversation with Van Delft. He walked across the road and looked in some more shop windows.

Fifteen minutes passed. Kirkpatrick looked at his watch again. There was a flower shop with flowers out on the street. He talked to the woman in the flower shop. 'Nice day.' 'Not too many people this morning.' 'Nice weather for October.' Kirkpatrick looked at his watch again. Then the door of *Lafon Jewellery* opened and Van Delft came out. He still had his black bag. Kirkpatrick didn't know what to say, but he felt the time was good.

'Erik!' he shouted across the street. 'Erik Van Delft!'

Van Delft turned and looked at Kirkpatrick. There was a question on his face. Kirkpatrick walked across the street to him, a big smile on his face.

'I saw you come out of that jeweller's,' Kirkpatrick said, 'and I knew it was you, man.'

Van Delft didn't say anything.

'You remember me, don't you?' said Kirkpatrick, still smiling. 'Lagos, Nigeria. Five years ago, no six maybe. We had some drinks together. You and I. We had a lot of drinks together!' Kirkpatrick laughed and put his hand out.

Van Delft took it and gave Kirkpatrick a small smile.

'Harley,' said Kirkpatrick. 'Harley Kirkpatrick. You know, man, this is a good day for me. And maybe it can be good for you too. Are you still in the business?' Kirkpatrick stood very near to Van Delft. 'You know, buying and selling? This and that?' He didn't wait for Van Delft's answer. He took a pen and paper out of his jacket, wrote a number and gave it to Van Delft. 'Here's my number, man. Call me. I know someone with good money. And he wants to buy.'

Van Delft looked at the paper and then at Kirkpatrick.

'Thank you, Mr Kirkpatrick,' he said.

'That's OK, man,' said Kirkpatrick. 'And it's Harley. Listen. I must go. It's good to see you again. Call me.'

Kirkpatrick turned and walked away.

Van Delft stood there in front of *Lafon Jewellery* and looked at the paper in his hand. Then he looked at Kirkpatrick and looked down at the paper again.

Chapter 3 *A second meeting*

Back at the *Daily Post*, Shepherd was in front of her computer. Kirkpatrick came in and she looked up.

'Well?' she asked.

'I met Van Delft,' he said.

'And?'

'I'm waiting,' replied Kirkpatrick, and he told Shepherd about his conversation with Van Delft.

'Harley!' said Shepherd, half shouting. 'He actually thinks you are going to buy some guns from him?' It was a kind of question.

'Well, yes. I think so.'

'Harley!' Shepherd was angry.

'It's going to be OK,' said Kirkpatrick. 'It's not stupid – it's very clever.'

Shepherd made an angry noise.

'Anyway,' said Kirkpatrick. 'We need to know more about Van Delft. And find out about *Lafon Jewellery*, too. That's L-A-F-O-N. It's a jeweller's shop on Hatton Garden. Van Delft was in there for about half an hour this morning.'

Shepherd did not say a word. She just worked at her computer.

Kirkpatrick walked across the room to his computer. He read some emails and answered them. After about an hour, Shepherd came over to his desk.

'Here's more on Van Delft and his business,' she said, and gave him some papers.

'Thanks,' said Kirkpatrick.

'Van Delft's ships come into Southampton, Amsterdam and other places in Europe,' said Shepherd. 'And . . . wait for it . . . they come from Angola, Liberia, Nigeria and some other African countries.'

'Countries with diamonds,' said Kirkpatrick.

'Yes,' said Shepherd. 'And guns are important in these countries too.'

Kirkpatrick didn't say anything for a minute. Then he looked at Shepherd.

'What about *Lafon Jewellery*?' he asked.

'I'm just starting to look for it on the Internet,' she said, and walked back across the room to her computer.

After about ten minutes Kirkpatrick's phone rang. He answered it.

'Kirkpatrick.'

'Van Delft here. I want to talk to you. Ten o'clock this evening. Be on the street in front of St Paul's Cathedral.'

The phone went dead.

'Yes!' thought Kirkpatrick. 'Now we're going to get a good story!'

He looked across the room but Shepherd wasn't there.

*   *   *

At ten to ten that evening Kirkpatrick was on the street near St Paul's Cathedral. He looked up at it, over 300 years old and very beautiful. Then he heard a car stop and the back door open.

'Kirkpatrick. Get in.'

Kirkpatrick looked into the car. Van Delft was in the back and a man was in the front.

Kirkpatrick got in the car and sat next to Van Delft.

'Drive,' said Van Delft to the man in the front. Van Delft looked at Kirkpatrick.

'Where are we going?' asked Kirkpatrick.

Van Delft smiled. 'Not far,' he said. 'Then we can have a little talk.'

They drove from St Paul's down to the river. There were always a lot of people here in the day, but at night it was very quiet. And at ten o'clock it was dark.

The car stopped.

'OK. Get out,' said Van Delft.

Kirkpatrick got out. Van Delft said something to the driver and then he got out too. The driver sat in the car.

'Come with me,' said Van Delft, going over to a little wall by the river. Kirkpatrick went after him. There were lights on the river. London Bridge was on the right, Tower Bridge on the left.

Van Delft looked down at the water. Then he turned to Kirkpatrick.

'I love London, you know. And I love Africa, too. I go there a lot.' Then he took out a gun.

'Oh no,' thought Kirkpatrick. 'Maybe this wasn't very clever.' But it was too late now.

'You know, we never met in Lagos.' Van Delft's eyes were cold.

'What are you talking about?' said Kirkpatrick. 'Of course we did, man. How do you think I know you?'

'That's a good question, Mr Kirkpatrick,' said Van Delft.

'You had a lot to drink that night, man,' said Kirkpatrick, 'and I did too, but I remember . . .'

'Stop!' said Van Delft. He put up one hand. 'Stop

talking. You must think I'm stupid. I never drink too much. I never forget anything. And we did not meet. Now, I'm telling you: don't come near me again.'

Just then Kirkpatrick heard a noise. He looked behind him but it was too late. The driver wasn't in the car now. He was behind Kirkpatrick with a baseball bat in his hands. Kirkpatrick tried to run but the bat hit him across the back. He went down on one knee and the bat hit him again. Then everything went dark.

Chapter 4 *Sophie Lafon*

Kirkpatrick opened his eyes slowly. Then he put his hands to his head. Ouch! His head hurt. Where was he? He looked at his watch. Two o'clock. Thursday morning. Ouch! His arms hurt. And his legs. He tried to sit up. Ouch! He was still near the river, but behind a wall.

Very slowly he got to his feet. He found some money in his jacket. He got up and walked slowly from behind the wall. The road was in front of him. He walked to the road and sat down. After about twenty minutes a taxi came down the street. Kirkpatrick stopped it.

'The *Daily Post*, Fleet Street,' he told the driver.

'You don't look good,' said the taxi driver.

'I don't feel good,' said Kirkpatrick.

The office was not far away and there was always someone there. Kirkpatrick sometimes worked all night on a big story and he always had some clothes there. He needed a wash. He felt dirty and he hurt all over.

In the bathroom at the *Daily Post* Kirkpatrick looked at his face and his body. His face wasn't too bad. But there were all kinds of interesting colours on his body: black, blue and purple. He had a wash, changed and got a coffee.

*   *   *

'Harley! What are you doing here?' It was Annie Shepherd. 'Why are you sleeping here?'

Kirkpatrick opened his eyes. He was in the coffee room. He looked at his watch. It was seven o'clock in the morning. He tried to stand up. His head still hurt.

'Ouch!'

So did his body.

'Harley, are you OK? What's wrong?'

'Van Delft,' said Kirkpatrick. 'He doesn't want to do business with me.' And he told Shepherd about his evening with Van Delft.

'I told you, Harley,' said Shepherd. 'I said don't do anything stupid!'

'OK, OK,' said Kirkpatrick. 'Anyway, we know he's here on business – he doesn't want me near him.'

'Yes,' said Shepherd, 'but we don't know where he is now.'

'What?'

'The person at the Charterhouse Hotel phoned me,' said Shepherd. 'That's why I came in. Van Delft left the hotel late yesterday evening.'

'We need to find him,' said Kirkpatrick. 'Did you find anything about *Lafon Jewellery*?'

'Yes,' said Shepherd. 'A Monsieur Bernard Lafon opened the shop in 1903. Today it's his granddaughter's. Her name's Sophie Lafon. She lives here in London and works in the London shop. There are also shops in Paris and Antwerp. They're hers too.'

'And?'

'That's it. The family are good jewellers. They buy and sell diamonds from all over the world.'

'Blood diamonds?'

'I don't know, but I don't think so.'

Kirkpatrick sat and thought. Shepherd watched him. Then he looked up and spoke.

'I'm going to talk to Sophie Lafon,' he said. 'She knows Van Delft. I think she knows where he is.'

'OK,' said Shepherd. 'And . . .'

'I know,' said Kirkpatrick. 'Don't do anything stupid.'

*   *   *

Kirkpatrick walked into *Lafon Jewellery*. A door at the back of the shop opened and a woman with long dark hair came into the room. Kirkpatrick thought she was in her thirties. She wore a black pullover and a short black skirt.

'Can I help you?' she asked.

'I'd like to speak to Sophie Lafon,' he said.

'I'm Sophie Lafon. And you are . . . ?'

'Harley Kirkpatrick. I'm a journalist for the *Daily Post*.'

'And why does a journalist want to talk to me?' There was a smile in her eyes.

'I'm working on a story about blood diamonds,' said Kirkpatrick.

Lafon stopped smiling.

'I never buy blood diamonds,' she said. 'Never.'

Kirkpatrick spoke again: 'A man came in here yesterday. His name is Erik Van Delft.'

'Yes,' she said. She watched his face. There was a question in her eyes.

'What can you tell me about him?' asked Kirkpatrick.

Lafon put her hands on the table in front of her.

'We buy diamonds from him sometimes,' she said. 'I know him a little.'

'Do you know where the diamonds are from?' asked Kirkpatrick.

'Of course,' said Lafon. 'There are always papers with diamonds. The papers say where the diamonds are from.'

'Did he sell you some diamonds yesterday?' asked Kirkpatrick quickly.

'Yes, he did.'

'Where were they from?'

'Africa. But why are you asking all these questions?'

'Does Van Delft sell blood diamonds?' asked Kirkpatrick.

Lafon's hand went up to her mouth.

'No!' she said. 'He can't . . . You can't . . . You can't think he is selling blood diamonds. To me?'

'I don't know,' said Kirkpatrick. 'But I want to find out. Are Van Delft's diamonds still here?'

'No,' replied Lafon. 'They're in Antwerp now.'

Kirkpatrick said nothing for a minute and thought.

'Blood diamonds,' said Lafon angrily. 'No, not Van Delft.'

'Where is he now?' asked Kirkpatrick.

'I don't know,' said Lafon. 'But . . .' she stopped.

'Yes?' asked Kirkpatrick.

'He's going to have some more diamonds for me this week or next,' said Lafon. She looked down at her hands and then up into Kirkpatrick's eyes.

'I want to help you,' she said. 'I hate blood diamonds.'

Kirkpatrick took a pen out of his jacket. He wrote his phone number and gave it to Sophie Lafon. 'Here,' he said. 'Call me when you know something – anything. Maybe I'm wrong, but some people think Van Delft buys and sells blood diamonds.'

Chapter 5 *Devon*

On Friday evening Kirkpatrick and Shepherd were still at work at six o'clock. Kirkpatrick thought it was time to go. He stood up. Just then his phone rang.

He answered it. 'Yes?'

'Is that Harley Kirkpatrick?' a woman's voice said quietly.

'Yes,' he replied.

'It's Sophie Lafon. I'm in Devon – Van Delft has a house here. I can't say much because he's in the next room.'

'OK.'

'Listen,' said Lafon. 'The house is in a place called Beesands. It's a very small place by the sea – just thirty or forty little houses. There is also one big white house. That's where Van Delft lives.'

'OK. Thanks,' said Kirkpatrick.

'And someone is coming here this evening with some more diamonds for me.'

'Who? What time?' asked Kirkpatrick.

'I must go,' said Lafon quickly. 'He's coming. Can you come down here?'

Kirkpatrick put the phone down.

'Annie,' Kirkpatrick called across the room. 'Van Delft's got a house in Devon. Somewhere called Beesands. I'm going to have a look at it.'

Shepherd stood up.

'I'm coming too,' she said. She put her small laptop computer in its bag and got her coat.

22

'You need help,' she said.

'It's all right,' said Kirkpatrick. 'I'm OK.'

'Come on, Harley.' Shepherd put her hand on Kirkpatrick's back.

'Ouch,' he said. His back still hurt.

'You're not OK,' said Shepherd. 'And I'm coming too.'

In the car Kirkpatrick told Shepherd about his conversation with Lafon. At ten thirty they got to Beesands.

It was easy to find Van Delft's house. There were some small houses on a road by the sea, and at the end of the road there was a big white house. It was easy to see because of the street lights. Kirkpatrick stopped the car about 250 metres away from the house. He and Shepherd sat and waited.

An old woman walked down the road and back. A door opened in one of the little houses and two dogs ran out. After five minutes the door opened again and someone called the dogs in. Some young men and women came out of a bar and started walking to their houses. There were lights in some of the windows in Van Delft's house.

Shepherd looked out over the sea. There were lights out at sea, too. White, red and green. Ships' lights. Shepherd closed her eyes. She thought for a minute or two. Then, she took out her laptop and her mobile phone, and got onto the Internet.

Kirkpatrick watched the house. New lights went on. The front door opened and closed.

He looked at Shepherd.

'I'm going to have a look at the house,' he said. Shepherd didn't say anything. Something on her computer was very interesting.

Kirkpatrick opened the door and got out of the car.

'I'm going to have a look at the house,' he said again. 'Back in five minutes.'

Still Shepherd didn't say anything. Maybe that was a good thing.

Kirkpatrick closed the door slowly and started walking up the road.

He walked quickly to the back of the house and saw two cars. The back door of one of the cars was open. Kirkpatrick got behind a tree. A man came out of the house. He put something in the car and went back in the house. It was Van Delft's driver – the man with the baseball bat.

Kirkpatrick waited and watched. Then he heard a noise. Quickly he looked behind him but it was too late. It was the driver. With a baseball bat.

And for the second time in thirty-six hours, everything went dark.

Chapter 6 *On the beach*

Kirkpatrick opened his eyes. His head hurt. He looked down. His hands were tied together. It was dark, but he could hear the sea. He must be on the beach. To his right was one of the cars from Van Delft's house. The driver was taking a long box from the back of the car. 'Guns,' thought Kirkpatrick. He looked at his watch. Eleven thirty. Then he heard someone behind him.

'Mr Kirkpatrick.' It was Van Delft. 'Good to see you.'

Van Delft walked in front of Kirkpatrick. He had a gun.

'Are there guns in the boxes?' said Kirkpatrick.

Van Delft smiled. But it was a cold smile.

'You are a very stupid man, Mr Kirkpatrick,' he said. 'Don't you listen? I said don't come near me again. And here you are. Yes, there are guns in the boxes. I bought them here in Britain.' He took some papers out of his jacket. 'These papers say they are going to a country in Asia, but they are not. They're going to a country in Africa. And that country is going to pay me a lot of money. In diamonds.'

'Blood diamonds?' asked Kirkpatrick.

'Yes, Mr Kirkpatrick, blood diamonds,' said Van Delft. 'That's why we're here on the beach. We don't want anybody to know about this.' He looked quickly at his watch. 'In about ten minutes someone is going to bring me the diamonds and take away these guns.'

Van Delft smiled again.

'And they're going to take you away too,' he said. 'You know too much now. They're going to take you and leave you in the sea somewhere. Somewhere far away.'

There were now ten boxes on the beach.

Just then Kirkpatrick heard a noise. He looked to his left and saw his car on the road near Van Delft's house. The car came onto the beach and started to drive over to them. Annie!

'What is she doing?' thought Kirkpatrick. He looked at Van Delft. Van Delft just stood and watched.

'So, Mr Kirkpatrick,' he said. 'There was someone down here with you.'

The car stopped in front of them. Kirkpatrick could now see two people in the car. The driver's door opened and Shepherd got out. The other door opened and a woman got out. Sophie Lafon! She had a gun in her hand. 'Go and sit with Kirkpatrick,' she said to Shepherd. Then to Van Delft,

'You were right, Erik. I found her in the car.'

'She can go for a long swim in the sea with her friend.' said Van Delft. 'Watch them. I'm going to help get the guns onto the beach.' He went to the car and took out a box.

'So it's you and Van Delft. You're working together,' said Kirkpatrick to Lafon. 'You know, you're very good. I didn't think of you two working together.'

'Of course, I am good,' said Lafon.

'And blood diamonds?' asked Kirkpatrick. 'You don't hate them after all?'

'Diamonds are diamonds, Mr Kirkpatrick,' said Lafon. 'And business is business.'

Kirkpatrick looked out to sea. There was a light out there. A small boat, he thought. A small boat coming from a big ship out at sea. Then the boat came near the beach and Kirkpatrick saw a man on it. The man shouted to Van Delft.

Chapter 7 *Guns and diamonds*

The boat was very near the beach now. Van Delft shouted back to the man in the boat. Van Delft's driver took one of the boxes down to the water. The man in the boat came and took the box back.

Kirkpatrick saw the man in the boat open the box. 'OK!' shouted the man.

He must be happy with the guns, thought Kirkpatrick.

'Harley.' It was Shepherd. But Lafon heard her.

'I said don't talk!' Lafon was angry.

The man came out of the boat with a small bag in his hand and started to walk through the water again. When he got to the beach, the man went to Van Delft and gave him the small bag. The driver came to get another box from the car.

Just then there was a lot of noise. Kirkpatrick looked to his left. There were four cars on the road near the beach, driving fast. The cars came down onto the beach and then there were blue lights.

Lafon saw them too.

'Look!' she shouted. 'Police!'

'Quick,' shouted Van Delft. The man and Van Delft ran into the water and quickly got into the boat. There was a noise and the boat started to go out to sea again.

Kirkpatrick was quick too. He stood up and took the gun from Lafon's hand. She didn't have time to stop him.

'OK,' he told her. 'Don't try and run. It's too late.'

The driver ran down the beach and into the sea. But the boat was now thirty metres away. He stopped and then came slowly back.

The police cars stopped and a policeman got out of the first car.

'Van Delft is on that boat,' said Kirkpatrick, 'with the diamonds.'

The policeman took out a phone and spoke into it for a short time.

Kirkpatrick looked out to sea. The sea was dark for a minute longer. He could just see Van Delft's boat. And then there were one, two, three blue lights on the sea. Police boats.

*   *   *

The police wanted to know everything. They asked a lot of questions and wanted answers to all of them. Shepherd and Kirkpatrick got away from Beesands at four in the morning.

'You drive,' said Kirkpatrick to Shepherd. 'And we need to get back quickly. We've got a good story here. Front page again, I think.'

Shepherd started the car. Kirkpatrick sat back and looked out of the window. He was very tired and his head hurt. He had some questions too. He looked at Shepherd.

'Thank you for calling the police, Annie,' he said. 'But why did you call them?'

Shepherd watched the road.

'The Internet,' she said. 'I found the names and times of ships going in and out of Southampton on the Internet. Three ships left Southampton yesterday evening, two of them going to Africa. Then I found the two ships on the Internet. And one of them was Erik Van Delft's.'

'I see,' said Kirkpatrick.

'I came up to the house to tell you,' said Shepherd. 'But you weren't there. Then I saw Van Delft and his driver put someone into the back of the car. I didn't know it was you but . . . then they drove onto the beach,' said Shepherd. 'And I knew everything. They had the guns in the car and the diamonds were on the ship. And it *was* you in the car – I knew it was. Then I went back and called the police.'

'Good work,' said Kirkpatrick and closed his eyes.

'Then Sophie Lafon came out of the house and ran over to me. She told me her name and of course I thought she was one of us, not a friend of Van Delft's and I . . . '

Shepherd looked at Kirkpatrick.

'Harley!' she said. 'Harley. Listen to me. Oh, OK. Go to sleep, then!'

Kirkpatrick was asleep with a smile on his face. Shepherd smiled too, and then she looked back at the road.